AMERICAN
TORAH TOONS

AMERICAN TORAH TOONS

54 illustrated commentaries

Lawrence Bush

JASON ARONSON INC.
Northvale, New Jersey
London

This book was set in 12 pt. Bodoni by Lawrence Bush.

10 9 8 7 6 5 4 3 2 1

Library of Congress Cataloging-in-Publication Data

Bush, Lawrence.
    American torah toons : 54 illustrated commentaries / Lawrence
Bush.
       p. cm.
    ISBN 0-7657-5972-1 (alk. paper)
    1. Bible. O.T. Pentateuch—Caricatures and cartoons.   I. Title.
BS1225.5.B87   1997
222'.106'0222—dc21

                                                                96-47020

Manufactured in the United States of America. Jason Aronson Inc. offers books and cassettes. For information and catalog write to Jason Aronson Inc., 230 Livingston Street, Northvale, New Jersey 07647.

Conceived in liberty,
and dedicated to
Susan

ACKNOWLEDGEMENTS

Some of these *American Torah Toons* appeared originally in *Babushkin's Digest,
Heaven Bone, Reconstructionism Today, Response, Tikkun,* and *Wealth & Covenant.*

Page 43, the photograph of Harriet Tubman by an anonymous photographer is
used with the permission of the Sophia Smith Collection, Smith College,
Northampton, MA.

Page 45, the photograph of the mountain of glasses is used with the permission
of the U.S. Holocaust Memorial Museum, Washington, DC.

Page 69, the model in the "Psychic Weightwatchers" ad is Ru Flynn (hugs and
kisses). The concept for the image is by Bruce Sager (ditto).

Page 73, the photograph of a defaced window is used with the permission of Yad
Vashem, Jerusalem, Israel.

Page 89, the photographs of Susan B. Anthony photo and Chief Joseph are used
with the permission of Culver Pictures, New York, NY.

Page 91, the photograph of the Woodstock Festival is by Ken Regan and originally appeared in Abbie Hoffman's *Woodstock Nation,* 1969.

Page 93, the still photograph from the film, *Heidi,* is used with the permission of
Culver Pictures, New York, NY. The photograph of the weeping survivor is used
with the permission of Yad Vashem, Jerusalem, Israel.

Page 101, the model in the "Intifadah" ad is Susan Griss.

Page 119, the hands in the photographs belong to Livia Vanaver. (Thanks!)

*Special thanks to Arthur Kurzweil, the Puffin Foundation, and all Babushkin's Digesters,
for their enthusiasm and encouragement.*

Introduction

Many years ago, my mom suggested that I write a bestseller. "You're smart and talented," she said, "and if you'd deign to read some of those books that sell millions of copies, I'm sure you could figure out how to create one!"

I'd already had one novel published and was struggling to turn my luck into lasting success. So I took Mom's advice. I went and read the biggest bestseller of all: the Bible.

It had all the right ingredients: sex, murder, family secrets, fantastic plot twists, exotic settings, epic battles, angels, etc. Something for everyone.

An easy read? No way. In fact, it took me years to read the whole book, let alone analyze the secrets of its commercial success. In the meantime, I found work as a writer and editor in the Jewish community. In keeping with that role, I began calling the Bible the Torah, and began learning and explaining to my friends the difference between Mishnah and Midrash, Aggadah and Akedah, Seder and Siddur.

Mostly, however, all they wanted was my expert advise on how to spell Ha-noo-ka. (Chanukah? Hanukkah? Hanuka?)

In light of their indifference to Jewish texts, I started to worry, along with the rest of the Jewish professional world, about "Jewish continuity." There was so much at stake: our prophetic tradition, our ancient heritage, our vast spiritual wisdom, our messianic dreams — not to mention our jobs!

The problem, I realized, is that the Torah, and Judaism itself, are simply "too much" for most people. Too much reading. Too much Hebrew. Too many patriarchs and beards. Too much God. Too many begats. Too many rules.

And not enough pictures.

Thus came my inspiration (notwithstanding Mom's advice to write a best-seller) to create *American Torah Toons* — illustrated commentaries on verses from each of the weekly "portions" into which Judaism divides the Torah.

In the name of Jewish continuity, I would try to create a sense of continuity between the archetypes, archaisms and arcana of the Torah and the daily realities of American life.

In the name of the Mishnah (the central compendium of Jewish law), which urges us to "turn it [the Torah] again and again, for everything is in it," I would turn the Torah upside down and inside out, bounce it on my knee and balance it on my head, tickle it and toss it in the air crying, "Whoopie!"

And in the name of popular demand, I would include a lot of pictures.

Lawrence Bush

Genesis

בראשית Genesis 1—6:8

"God said, 'Let there be lights in the expanse of the sky
to separate day from night; they shall serve as signs for
the set times — the days and the years; and they shall
serve as lights in the expanse of the sky to shine upon
the earth.' And it was so. God made the two great lights,
the greater light to dominate the day and the lesser light
to dominate the night, and the stars. And God set them
in the expanse of the sky to shine upon the earth, to
dominate the day and the night, and to separate light
from darkness. And God saw that this was good."

Shofar

At this very moment, the earth is hurtling through space at $18^1/_2$ miles per second!

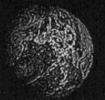

The rest of our expanding universe is rushing outwards at speeds ranging up to thousands of miles per second — zillions of stars and other heavenly bodies, both vast and tiny!

Meanwhile, our planet rotates on its axis at a speed of over 1,000 miles per hour, allowing us all to receive the life-giving rays of the sun — which burns with a surface temperature of 10,000°!

And here we sit, safe and sound

And ready to blow our horns!

נח   Genesis 6:9—11

"The earth became corrupt before God; the earth was
filled with lawlessness."

Conglomeration

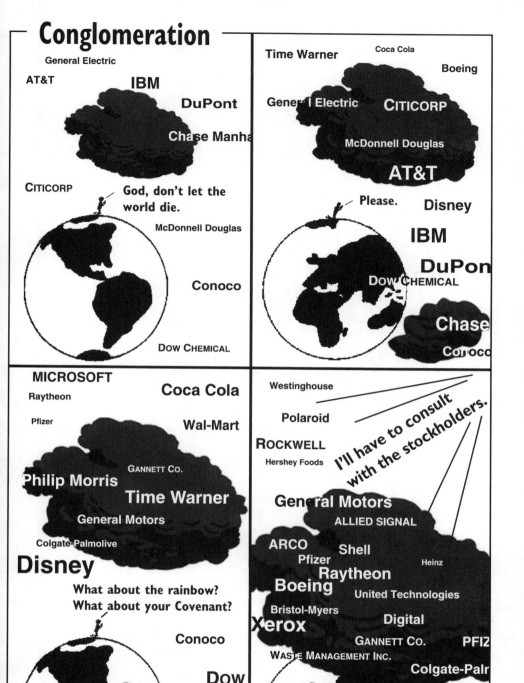

General Electric

AT&T

IBM

DuPont

Chase Manha[ttan]

CITICORP

God, don't let the world die.

McDonnell Douglas

Conoco

Dow Chemical

Time Warner

Coca Cola

Boeing

General Electric

CITICORP

McDonnell Douglas

AT&T

Please.

Disney

IBM

DuPon[t]

Dow Chemical

Chase

Conoco

MICROSOFT

Raytheon

Pfizer

Coca Cola

Wal-Mart

Gannett Co.

Philip Morris

Time Warner

General Motors

Colgate-Palmolive

Disney

What about the rainbow?
What about your Covenant?

Conoco

Dow

Du Pont

Chase Manhattan

General Electric

IBM

Westinghouse

Polaroid

Rockwell

Hershey Foods

I'll have to consult with the stockholders.

General Motors

Allied Signal

ARCO

Pfizer

Shell

Heinz

Raytheon

Boeing

United Technologies

Bristol-Myers

Digital

Xerox

Gannett Co.

PFIZ[ER]

Waste Management Inc.

Colgate-Palm[olive]

Ford

MICROSOFT

Conoco

CITICOR[P]

Disney

Coca Cola

AT&T

Chase

Du P[ont]

Time Warner

5

לֶךְ-לְךָ   Genesis 12—17

"The Lord said to Abram, 'Go forth from your native land and from your father's house to the land that I will show you . . .'"

God and Dog

Everything was man-made and bizarre. New York seemed accursed, like Sodom. Maybe my feelings were a matter of personal paranoia — yet the sense of "right" and "wrong" I had about city life had a force of religious conviction, of "knowing."

When I lived in the city, I couldn't find God.

When I got a dog, my need to return to nature became irresistible. So we moved to the country. . .

. . . where every time I step out the door I declare, "My God!"

Barukh atah adonai eloheynu melekh ha-olam shehekheyanu vekiyemanu vehigianu lazeman hazeh

(Sometimes I worry that my spirituality brands me as a pagan. Most Jews I know don't live in the country or own dogs. But I don't worry about it too much.)

Then, last winter, my dog Malka was killed on the road by a snow plow.

I wailed and wept. Why? Why?

God seemed absent again.

Months later, when my wife was discussing theology with the kids, our 7-year-old son said he had felt close to God "when Malka died and Poppy (that's me) cried."

We'll be getting another dog soon.

וירא   Genesis 18—22

"They arrived at the place of which God had told him. Abraham built an altar there; he laid out the wood; he bound his son Isaac; he laid him on the top of the altar, on top of the wood. And Abraham picked up the knife to slay his son. Then an angel of the Lord called to him from heaven: 'Abraham! Abraham!' And he answered, 'Here I am.'"

Akedah

Last year we took our kids down to Florida* for the High Holidays via Amtrak. It was a 30-hour trip — pretty awful.

*not to Disney World

The worst part was the young couple seated right behind us. They had a baby girl and a 4-year-old boy, and they were terrible, abusive parents.

They had no notion of what was age-appropriate behavior. They had brought nothing to entertain their son: no crayons, books or games, for a 2,000-mile journey.

In fact, the boy was remarkably well-behaved and self-possessed. But the parents kept hissing at him and slapping his hands, his arms, his butt, his head, wherever they could reach, for no reason.

The mother even scolded and shook the baby a few times for "making noise."

I wanted desperately to intercede, beyond setting a good example and sharing our own kids' crayons and stuff. Maybe for starters I could go have a beer with the father (who had polished off a couple of bottles as soon as they got on the train) and talk with him about how challenging parenting can be . . .

— ABRAHAM! ABRAHAM!

"Susan," I said to my wife, "if we can't do anything about this situation in the seat right behind us, what hope is there for political and spiritual transformation on the larger scale?"

"They'll resent you and think you're a meddler," Susan cautioned me.

"And then they'll take it out on their kids."

WHERE, O WHERE IS THERE AN ANGEL
WHEN YOU NEED ONE?

9

חיי שרה Genesis 23—25:18

"Raising her eyes, Rebekah saw Isaac. . . . (S)he took her veil and covered herself. The servant told Isaac all the things that he had done. Isaac then brought her into the tent of his mother Sarah, and he took Rebekah as his wife."

Canaanite Women:
A Pictorial

It took me years to fully recognize
Susan's humanity.

Even after we'd travelled
far and wide together,
made love on mountainsides and beaches . . .

Even after we were living together,
sharing a bed, a toilet, a refrigerator . . .

Still, I was ruled by images of some
ultimately desirable woman,
who never had chapped lips or a pimple on her chin,
and was always turned on and waiting for me . . .

Finally, one night, I had a dream.
It was after a dinner party, during which I'd felt hypercritical of Susan.
I had gone to bed alienated, dissatisfied, poisoned.

In my dream, she and I were again visiting friends.
We arrived at their house, and I immediately started scouring
the foyer bookshelves and cabinets for *Playboy* magazines!
I was literally on my knees, looking through drawers — no *Playboy* !
Standing next to me — Susan.

We dashed off to the next house! I searched high and low for
Playboy. Nowhere to be found!
Standing next to me — Susan.

On to the next house. I tore the place apart — no *Playboy*!
Standing next to me — Susan.

At last I woke up.
Sleeping next to me — Susan.

תולדת   Genesis 25:19—28:9

"Once when Jacob was cooking a stew, Esau came in from
the open, famished. And Esau said to Jacob, 'Give me
some of that red stuff to gulp down, for I am famished'
. . . Jacob said, 'First sell me your birthright.' And Esau
said, 'I am at the point of death, so of what use is my
birthright to me?' . . . Thus did Esau spurn the birthright."

Synthesis

My parents were Communists.

My brother became a Christian.

I am a Jew without a beard.

They taught, "Religion is the opiate of the people."

He asked, "Where can I get some?"

I got high with a little help from my friends.

They believed in the inevitable fall of capitalism.

He believes in the fallen nature of humankind.

I believe whoever hugs me.

Their plan was for a classless communist society.

His plan is for salvation and an everlasting state of grace.

My plan is never to die.

וַיֵּצֵא   Genesis 28:10—32:3

"He had a dream; a ladder was set on the ground and its
top reached to the sky, and angels of God were going up
and down on it. . . . Jacob awoke from his sleep and
said, 'Surely the Lord is present in this place, and I did
not know it!' Shaken, he said, 'How awesome is this
place! This is none other than the abode of God, and
that is the gateway to heaven.'"

Angels

Cookies-and-milk time! I ask my kids what they're learning in school these days. "The food chain," Zoe says. "And what's that?" I ask. So she explains.

"I can think of another kind of food chain," I suggest to them. "Take those cookies, for instance . . ."

"Okay!" they shout, each grabbing another.

"Now, think about how many people are involved in getting you those cookies . . ." As I list them — the farmers, chemists, bakers, package makers, factory owners, trucker drivers, supermarket workers, me, their mom, the people who pay our wages — my children's eyes seem to light up with unusual excitement.

"In fact," I add exuberantly, "I bet you at any moment in the day, even when you're completely alone, there are at least a hundred other people involved with you. If you just look around the room, you'll be able to see them."

"Cool," Jonah says.

"Dad?" Zoe asks.

"Yes?"

"Could we have *another* cookie?"

Hmm . . .

"Okay," I agree. . .

— "only let's first say a blessing, so all those people can hear it, okay?"

"Barukh atah yah, eloheynu ruakh ha-olam, boray meenay meezonot!"

וישלח   Genesis 32:4—36

"Now Dinah, the daughter whom Leah had borne to Jacob, went out to visit the daughters of the land. Shechem son of Hamor the Hivite, chief of the country, saw her, and took her and lay with her by force."

Anne Frank
Has Second Thoughts

"It's really a wonder that I haven't dropped all my ideals, because they seem so absurd and impossible to carry out. Yet I keep them, because in spite of everything I still believe that people are really good at heart."

"On the other hand, maybe people are just a bunch of dirtbags — *farshunk-eneh paskudnyakim. Nu? Nu? Azoy is es! Me lost nit leben!*"

וישב Genesis 37—40

"And much as she coaxed Joseph day after day, he did not yield to her request to lie beside her, to be with her."

Anti-Nuclear Agitation

After 18 years of marriage, things had gotten pretty nuclear in our family, despite our '60s ethic . . .

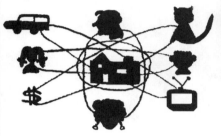

We were in a small after-hours group, flirting and drinking and talking kind of abstractly about relationships, but I took the plunge and asked her, *sotto voce,* if she felt like taking me up to her room then and there.

She didn't say no — but when she left a little while later, we didn't even kiss goodbye.

Still, I felt agitated for days after the conference. My whole life seemed like an obligation!

Until one night, when I was away from home at a conference, and this really elegant artist said . . .

Moi?

. . . that she could think of a lot of women who'd be interested in having an affair with me!

I began daydreaming about old girlfriends, about all the women I'd been attracted to over the course of 18 years.

If Mick Jagger, Wilt Chamberlain and other famous men could have thousands upon thousands of lovers, why couldn't I have two or three? I began making declarations to my friends that monogamy was an unnatural condition.

They all agreed — except my wife. After a week of my brooding, she rolled me over one night and we had a really hot time of it.

In the morning, the kids came into bed with us.

"Isn't this nice?" my wife said.

I had to agree. Most of the people I know who sleep around are really quite lonely!

מִקֵּץ   Genesis 41—44:17

"And Joseph said to Pharaoh, 'Pharaoh's dreams are one and the same: God has told Pharaoh what He is about to do. The seven healthy cows are seven years, and the seven healthy ears are seven years; it is the same dream. . . . Immediately ahead are seven years of great abundance in all the land of Egypt . . .'"

On Sale This Week!

EXTRA! LOW PRICES — JOE — PLUS THE FRIENDLIEST SERVICE IN TOWN!

Instant **Renewal** ® 3-Lb. Box **99**¢	Assorted **Explanations** **2**³⁹ Mix 'n'Match! lb.	**Belly Laughs** guaranteed fresh **69**¢
Pure Pleasure Limit One per Customer **49**¢	**Thighs & Loins** Family Pac **79**¢	Multi-Purpose **Dough 89**¢
Imagination As seen on television Bunch **2**⁴⁹	Premium **Guts 49**¢	**Space 79**¢
Insights **1**²⁹ Choose from a wide variety of designer styles 6-pack	**Authenticity** **1**²⁹	Unconditional **Love 69**¢

Buy One, Get One Free! Imported **Romance** with this coupon **2**⁹⁹ Frozen	**Buy One, Get One Free!** *Satisfaction* with this coupon **1**⁷⁹ while it lasts	*Manager's Special* **Attention** with this coupon **1**⁸⁸ undivided

וַיִּגַּשׁ   Genesis 44:18—47:27

"They went up from Egypt and came to their father
Jacob in the land of Canaan. And they told him, 'Joseph
is alive; yes, he is ruler over the whole land of Egypt.'
His heart went numb, for he did not believe them. But
when they recounted all that Joseph had said to them,
and when he saw the wagons that Joseph had sent to
transport him, the spirit of their father Jacob revived.
'Enough!' said Israel. 'My son Joseph is still alive! I
must go and see him before I die.' "

Missing in Action

There are ten men in the jacuzzi at our Jewish men's retreat. The facilitator suggests that we begin our session by going in turn, each of us to conjure up an image of our father and to ask him aloud — here, amidst this naked minyan — a question never before asked.

I glibly volunteer to go first. My dad, after all, has been dead for 13 years, and I have mourned and dreamed and written about him extensively. Yet as soon as my question pops into mind — "So what do you think of my children?" — my throat chokes and eyes fill with tears.

One by one, the others follow.
"Who are you?" "What do you really think of me?" "Why did you always seem unhappy?" "Did you love Mom?" Such elementary questions — we are so ignorant of our fathers' feelings!

They were too busy working, too busy fixing, too busy napping, too busy being angry.

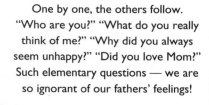

I look around the *mikveh* at the chests and shoulders, the beards and manes, of these men — mature men, accomplished men, professional men, articulate men.

And I see us as a circle of mighty oaks, full of trunk and foliage and skywards splendor, but with shallow roots — so shallow that we can barely keep ourselves upright.

"Our fathers," I declare to the group, "were all missing in action."

"Yeah," says another, "and we were the rescue squad!"

"But all we can do is rescue ourselves," says the facilitator.

"Amen," the other mutters.

"Amen," I agree, splashing water on my face, meanwhile thinking, *Oh, man, oh, man, oh, man* . . .

ויחי   Genesis 47:28—50

"And when the time approached for Israel to die, he
summoned his son Joseph and said to him, 'Do me this
favor, place your hand under my thigh as a pledge of
your steadfast loyalty: please do not bury me in
Egypt.' "

He Keeps It Out of Sight

When I was about 11 years old and had been studying classical guitar for a couple of years, my mom suggested that I learn my dad's favorite song, "Mack the Knife," from *The Threepenny Opera*.

So I did. It was a little tricky, too. My first barre chords, my first jazzy strumming, and my first stab at arranging — though I wasn't sure if my dad would prefer a swinging Bobby Darin version or the organ-grinder feeling of the Weil-Blitzstein original.

Finally, I could play the chords without difficulty, had all the words memorized, and could sing them without botching up my playing. One evening, I entered my parents' bedroom, where Dad was sitting alone, reading.

I played the song, a so-so performance. He nodded thoughtfully, sighed and said: "That's the song I'd like played at my funeral."

"Okay," I said, with a little laugh, and left the room.

Mom saw me in the foyer. "What did he think?" she asked.

I didn't want to answer. I felt as if my dad had confessed something that I could tell no one else — as if I had seen the man naked and now held all his secrets in my hand.

"He liked it," I said.

OH THE SHARK HAS PRETTY TEETH, DEAR

Just a jacknife has MacHeath, dear, and he keeps it out of

Sukie Tawdry, Jenny Diver, Polly Beachum

The cement's just for the weight, dear

For years after, I would recite the words of that song in my head, trying to pry open my dad's inner life. "Mack the Knife" came to embody every secret sin and underground desire that marked his masculinity, made him cool, kept him aloof, and frustrated the fucking hell out of him.

It also came to embody the gulf between us. What could a boy-child offer to a man like Mack the Knife?

Finally, when he died at age 70, I told my mother and brother of his request. I said it kind of nonchalently, as if it were just another arrangement detail. And so . . .

As our friends and family members settled into the funeral parlor with their eyes on the casket, they heard the balladeer from the Lotte Lenya record singing: "Just a jacknife has MacHeath, dear, and he keeps it . . ."

And when Jenny Diver cried, "Look! There goes Mack, the Knife!" they all heard me bawling, "Hoo, hoo!" as the balladeer ushered my father away with: ". . . Out . . . of . . . sight."

Exodus

שמות Exodus 1—6:1

" 'Look, the Israelite people are much too numerous for us. Let us deal shrewdly with them, so that they may not increase . . .' "

35,000 Robert Cantors

The first important thing I remember watching on television was the Eichmann trial in 1961.

At school we'd spend time thinking up ways for him to be tortured and executed.

String him up by his balls!

Pierce his skin with six million pins until he bleeds to death!

They should cart him around in a cage and people can spit or do whatever they want to him.

There were about 30 kids in my 4th grade class. Most of them were Jewish — we lived in a Jewish neighborhood.

I remember there were two Linda's and two David's in the class — but let's keep it simple and say there were 30 kids with 30 different names.

There'd have to be 35,000 of each of them — 35,000 Becky Silvers (real cute and sparkly), 35,000 Arnold Glicksteins (a klutz), 35,000 Sandi Meislers (snooty, but I liked her), 35,000 Reba Wertheimers (a brain), 35,000 Robert Cantors (my best friend) — 35,000 of each of them, to come even close to the number of Jewish kids Adolf Eichmann sent to the gas chambers in three or four years.

Me

And I knew that he never shed a tear, not even afterwards, because, like I told Robert, if the guy's heart had opened even a crack, he would've had to commit suicide!

וארא   Exodus 6:2—9

"I have now heard the moaning of the Israelites because
the Egyptians are holding them in bondage, and I have
remembered My covenant."

Dayenu

"For we were slaves unto Pharaoh in Egypt. . ."

"In every generation, you ought to regard yourself as though you had personally come out of Egypt. . ."

"And the more we tell of the departure, the more we are to be praised. . ."

Tough winter, huh?

You can say that again.

31

בֹּא   Exodus 10—13:16

"None of you shall go outside the door of his house until morning. For when the Lord goes through to smite the Egyptians, He will see the blood on the lintel and the two doorposts, and the Lord will pass over the door and not let the Destroyer enter and smite your home."

The Face

Take cover, class.
Under your desks.
Face away from
the window.

בשלח   Exodus 13:17—17

"In Your love You lead the people You redeemed; / In Your strength You guide them to Your holy abode. / The peoples hear, they tremble; / Agony grips the dwellers in Philistia. / Now are the clans of Edom dismayed; / The tribes of Moab — trembling grips them; / All the dwellers in Canaan are aghast. / Terror and dread descend upon them; / Through the might of Your arm they are as still as stone — / Till Your people cross over, O Lord, / Till Your people cross whom You have ransomed."

At My Seder Table

This is Harriet Tubman, as she appeared in her forties during the Civil War. She was a spy, nurse and fighter for the Union Army.

By that time, she had already made 19 trips into the South in a 10-year period (1850-1860), during which she led some 300 slaves to freedom on the "Underground Railroad."

Her career began with her own escape from slavery, which led her to realize

> I was free, but there was no one to welcome me to the land of freedom. I was a stranger in a strange land, and my home after all was down in the old cabin quarter, with the old folks and my brothers and sisters. But to this solemn resolution I came: I was free, and they should be free also; I would make a home for them in the North, and the Lord helping me, I would bring them all there.

Harriet Tubman did just that, rescuing her elderly parents and nearly all of her 10 siblings. Not one of her "passengers" was ever lost to captors.

> I had reasoned this out in my mind; there was one of two things I had a right to, liberty or death. If I could not have one, I would have the other; for no man should take me alive. I should fight for my liberty as long as my strength lasted, and when the time came for me to go, the Lord would let them take me.

Slave owners posted a $40,000 reward for her capture, dead or alive.

She lived to be 93.

יתרו Exodus 18—20

"On the third day, as morning dawned, there was thunder, and lightning, and a dense cloud upon the mountain, and a very loud blast of the horn; and all the people who were in the camp trembled. Moses led the people out of the camp toward God, and they took their places at the foot of the mountain."

Leibowitz's Mountain

Every once in a while, you glimpse a pattern in nature, the way the microcosmic and macrocosmic overlap,
or you just admire a vividly colored flower, attended by a buzzing bee, and you think,
Surely there's a Creator for all this!

Soon after, a typhoon kills 2,000 people in Bangladesh . . .

Every once in a while, you wonder about the redemptive power of history, how individual and social reality interplay in these complex, mysterious ways,

how mass consciousness seems to reach a critical point and -zap!- justice wins out! And you think,
This must all be leading somewhere!

Then 200,000 people get hacked to death in Rwanda . . .

Every once in a while, something happens that arrests your attention, unbottles your feelings, and grants you an opportunity for tremendous insight and personal growth, and you think,
None of this is coincidental!

Then you find your car scratched and dented in a shopping mall parking lot . . .

Every once in a while, a work of art strikes you as more real than any fact, and the line between reality and metaphor suddenly is a dotted line, and you think,
The reality of God is really up to me!

Then a microscopic virus causes you to throw up all night long . . .

So what's left to you? Six hundred and thirteen mitzvot, take it or leave it.

משפטים   Exodus 21—24

"He who insults his father or his mother shall be put to
death."

MY
LT

תרומה   Exodus 25—27:19

"The Lord spoke to Moses, saying: Tell the Israelite
people to bring Me gifts; you shall accept gifts for Me
from every person whose heart so moves him. And
these are the gifts you shall accept from them: gold,
silver and copper; blue, purple, and crimson yarns, fine
linen, goats' hair; tanned ram skins, dolphin skins, and
acacia wood; oil for lighting, spices for the anointing oil
and for the aromatic incense; lapis lazuli and other
stones for setting, for the ephod and for the breastpiece.
And let them make Me a sanctuary that I may dwell
among them. Exactly as I show you — the pattern of the
Tabernacle and the pattern of all its furnishings — so
shall you make it."

Gift-Giving

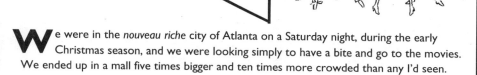

We were in the *nouveau riche* city of Atlanta on a Saturday night, during the early Christmas season, and we were looking simply to have a bite and go to the movies. We ended up in a mall five times bigger and ten times more crowded than any I'd seen.

Shopping malls always fill me with visions of dystopia and feelings of dread. I become a stranger in a strange land, in which human culture has been homogenized into brand names, human desire flattened into acquisitiveness, human fraternity reduced to people-ogling — all within a windowless, nature-free landscape.

This place was even worse than most, crawling with shoppers, the service workers desperate to keep up . . . I was thinking, *Saturday night in hell,* when lo, amidst the burger and taco counters, I spotted a healthy-looking salad bar.

It was staffed by a Latin American guy dressed in an absurd uniform. assembling several meals while listening to other people's orders. ich order right, gave generous portions, and *never stopped smiling.*

At five bucks an hour, the man was radiant.

When our turn came, I told him, "You sure do your job well." "I like serving all these nice people," he replied, ringing us up.

After our meal (really not bad), I called the movie theater — which turned out to be in a *different* giant mall across the boulevard. Three times the pay phone rejected my quarter. Each time I cursed — only to find an extra quarter in the coin return box. "Manna," Susan observed, which set me to laughing so hard that I couldn't hear the recorded message, and we spent the rest of our evening right there in the mall, buying Hanukah gifts.

תצוה   Exodus 27:20—30:10

"Then take two lazuli stones and engrave on them the names of the sons of Israel: six of their names on the one stone, and the names of the remaining six on the other stone, in the order of their birth. . . . as stones for remembrance of the Israelite people, whose names Aaron shall carry upon his two shoulderpieces for remembrance before the Lord."

Multihorticulturalism

כי תשא　Exodus 30:11—34

"And all the people took off the gold rings that were in
their ears and brought them to Aaron. This he took
from them and cast in a mold and made it into a molten
calf. And they exclaimed, 'This is your god, O Israel,
who brought you out of the land of Egypt!' When Aaron
saw this, he built an altar before it; and Aaron an-
nounced: 'Tomorrow shall be a festival of the
Lord!' Early next day, the people offered up burnt
offerings and brought sacrifices of well-being; they sat
down to eat and drink, and then rose to dance."

Mad-nna

THIS IS MAD-NNA,
AMERICAN GODDESS,
AND SHE
IS SO POWERFUL,
AND TALENTED,
AND RICH,
AND UBIQUITOUS,
AND PROTEAN,
AND SEXY,
AND RISQUÉ,
AND OUTTASITE,
THAT
I DARE NOT
EVEN PRESENT
HER FULL IMAGE
LEST I BE
SUED
UNTO DEATH!

SHE'S MY IDOL.
I WORSHIP HER.
MAD-NNA.

ויקהל Exodus 35—38:20

"They made the planks for the Tabernacle of acacia wood, upright. The length of each plank was ten cubits, the width of each plank a cubit and a half."

The Tabernacle

"They call this forest 'Nature's Cathedral,' " I read from the guidepost display.

"What's a cathedral?" asked Zoë, my daughter.

"A giant church," I explained.

"These trees are Christian?"

"No, of course not. But I tell you," I said as an aside to my wife, Susan, "we're not the only beings on this earth made in God's image!"

I went on reading as we waited for Zoë's brother to complete his walk along the 300-foot length of a fallen redwood. "They're unique to North America," I reported. "From the base to the treetop there are three different climatic zones. But their roots — listen to this — their roots are only six to ten feet deep!"

"Why don't they topple over?" Susan wondered.

"Their roots," I reported, "spread out 80 feet and intertwine with the roots of other redwoods."

"My God, they're holding hands under the ground!" Susan said, and laughed with delight.

Zoë, who had sort of stopped listening, cried, "Look!" She was pointing directly overhead. "The trees are making a Jewish star."

פקודי   Exodus 38:21—40

"All the gold that was used for the work, in all of the
sanctuary — the elevation offering of gold — came to 29
talents and 730 shekels by the sanctuary weight. The silver
of those of the community who were recorded came to 100
talents and 1,775 shekels by sanctuary weight: a half-
shekel a head, half a shekel by the sanctuary weight, for
each one who was entered in the records . . ."

The Torah of Money

Five Jews were playing *dreidl* at Hanukah time. One of them held up a piece of money and asked: "What is the true essence of a coin?"

"Its sheen," suggested one. "If you preserve it through the years from wear and tear, the coin's value grows."

"Its two-sidedness," said the second. "With a single flip, you can settle quarrels and decide about the future."

"Its weight," observed the third. "The heftier the coin, the more it can lighten your burdens."

"Its engravings," said the fourth. "Study those and you can understand the values of the whole society."

The one who had asked now walked to the window and handed the coin to a poor person on the street, then said:

"The essence of a coin is its shape. A coin is like a wheel — it's meant to move around."

Leviticus

וַיִּקְרָא   Leviticus 1—5

"If his offering to the Lord is a burnt offering of birds, he shall choose his offering from turtledoves or pigeons. The priest shall bring it to the altar, pinch off its head, and turn it into smoke on the altar; and its blood shall be drained out against the side of the altar. He shall remove its crop with its contents, and cast it into the place of the ashes, at the east side of the altar. The priest shall tear it open by its wings, without severing it, and turn it into smoke on the altar, upon the wood that is on the fire. It is a burnt offering, an offering by fire, of pleasing odor to the Lord."

Burnt Offering

Eighteen years ago, on the morning of our wedding. . .

I was sitting at my desk, working on our vows . . .

There was a sudden scurrying on the floor.
I looked just in time to see a small bird making its death squeal —
a terrified cry, beak wide open, wings outstretched — before my cat pounced again.

I shrieked. The cat ran out through the window
with his offering.

When I mention this incident, friends *kibbitz* me about it as a marriage omen.
Not so — our marriage was *bashert* (meant to be), and we will remain married . . .

until death.

צַו   Leviticus 6—8

"This is the ritual of the guilt offering: it is most holy."

B'Tselem Elohim (in God's Image)

At least once a day, I become aware of how I've short-changed someone in my interactions.

Usually it's because I'm goal-oriented and rushing. People are then objects to me — whether obstacles or tools, it doesn't matter.

Most often it's my own children who offer opportunities that I squander. Unlike grownups, who are satisfied to deal with me as an object in their paths, my kids are present-tense and emotional in their orientation. I disappoint them a lot.

How do I become aware of this each day? Someone makes themselves human to me, usually inadvertently — with a flashing look, a smile, an extra word of engagement, whatever. Suddenly, the cardboard figure is a breathing being — the It is a Thou — and I am summoned.

There is always a pang of regret — how could I have slept so long? But mostly I feel grateful for the awakening!

"Barukh atah adonay eloheynu khey ha'olamim hama'avir shenah me'eynay utnumah me'afapay."

55

שמיני   Leviticus 9-11

"These are the instructions concerning animals, birds, all living creatures that move in water, and all creatures that swarm on earth, for distinguishing between the unclean and the clean, between the living things that may be eaten and the living things that may not be eaten."

McWorld

תזריע   Leviticus 12-13

"When a woman at childbirth bears a male, she shall be
unclean seven days; she shall be unclean as at the time
of her menstrual infirmity. —On the eighth day the
flesh of his foreskin shall be circumcised. — She shall
remain in a state of blood purification for thirty-three
days: she shall not touch any consecrated thing, nor
enter the sanctuary until her period of purification is
completed."

The
Way
It
Was
Done

This is my mom and dad, a few years before my birth. He's in uniform, she's in slacks. The baby boom is just around the corner.

Mom was drugged and only semi-conscious when I was born. I was bottle-fed from the start. "That's the way it was done," she says. I was named in advance, after no one in particular.

Dad was chain-smoking and reading in the waiting room while I was born. He was home, sleeping, when the doctor circumcised me.

Rumor has it that I was a happy, healthy child . . .

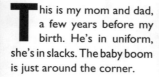

But sometimes, for no particular reason, I just feel out of touch with my life!

מצרע   Leviticus 14-15

"Such shall be the ritual for him who has a scaly affection and whose means for his cleansing are limited."

Wasps!

I was sitting and reading, minding my own business, at this place I consider to be "my" spot — a tiny little stream that no one seems to know about . . .

All of a sudden, I was attacked by wasps!

They must have been nested in the muddy bank of the stream. I don't think I even stepped on them — I was just sitting, reading! — but I got seven or eight stings and had to run for my life!

Fifteen minutes later, as their venom spread through my body, every old injury, rash or infection I'd ever sustained made a comeback, erupting all over me. It was astounding how my body remembered it all!

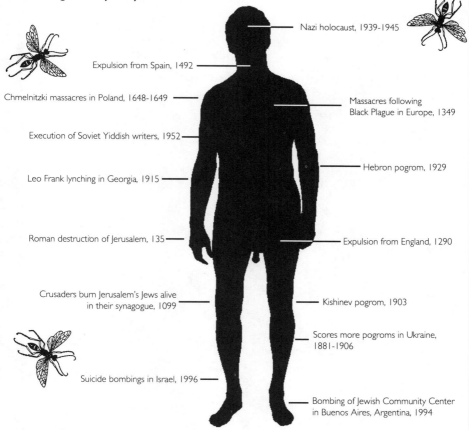

Nazi holocaust, 1939-1945

Expulsion from Spain, 1492

Chmelnitzki massacres in Poland, 1648-1649

Massacres following Black Plague in Europe, 1349

Execution of Soviet Yiddish writers, 1952

Hebron pogrom, 1929

Leo Frank lynching in Georgia, 1915

Roman destruction of Jerusalem, 135

Expulsion from England, 1290

Crusaders burn Jerusalem's Jews alive in their synagogue, 1099

Kishinev pogrom, 1903

Scores more pogroms in Ukraine, 1881-1906

Suicide bombings in Israel, 1996

Bombing of Jewish Community Center in Buenos Aires, Argentina, 1994

Luckily, I'm not allergic! I fought back with a little antihistamine, and I went back to "my" spot the very next day. (My book was still there, too.) Ain't no wasps gonna drive me away for long!

אחרי מות   Leviticus 16—18

"For on this day atonement shall be made for you to
cleanse you of all your sins; you shall be clean before
the Lord. It shall be a sabbath of complete rest for you,
and you shall practice self-denial; it is a law for all
time."

Life got you down?

Get with the program!

Psychic Weight Watchers

Lighten Up!

קדשים   Leviticus 19-20

"If a man lies with a male as one lies with a woman, the two of them have done an abhorrent thing; they shall be put to death — their bloodguilt is upon them."

Niemöller
on the Capitol Steps

In America they came first for the faggots with AIDS,
and I didn't speak up because I wasn't a faggot with AIDS.
Then they came for the crack-heads,
and I didn't speak up because I wasn't a crack-head.
Then they came for the welfare chiselers,
and I didn't speak up because I wasn't a welfare chiseler.
Then they came for the baby killers,
and I didn't speak up because I wasn't a
baby killer.
Then they came for the urban underclass,
and I didn't speak up because I wasn't
in the urban underclass.
Then they came for the godless
liberals,
and I didn't speak up
because I wasn't a
godless liberal.
Then they came fo

אמר   Leviticus 21—24

"'And when you reap the harvest of your land, you shall not reap all the way to the edges of your field, or gather the gleanings of your harvest; you shall leave them for the poor and the stranger: I the Lord am your God.'"

Hamburger Helper

While the kids were attending their karate class, I went shopping at Shoprite. We were hosting a seder that weekend for ten people — plus my daughter had decided to become a vegetarian and we were, in general, feeling hard-pressed to feed her.

So I did one hell of a shop.

(After all, the Jerusalem Talmud says we'll all be held accountable in the hereafter for every fruit that we saw but did not taste. Who am I to spurn God's blessings?)

By the time I reached the check-out, I was fixing to be late for the kids. . .

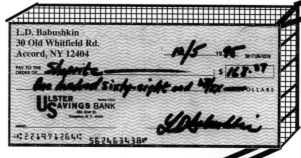

Yikes, two fully-loaded shopping carts ahead of me!

I spent my time thumbing through *People* magazine and wondering what it would be like to have a cook and a maid and never have to spend time waiting on line.

Then a couple joined the line behind me. Their shopping cart had may be fifteen items, which I scanned with a glance: big loaf of bread, potatoes, whole chicken, generic toilet paper, Shoprite sugar cookies, chunk light tuna, Shoprite mayo, chopmeat, a box of Hamburger Helper. . .

The people themselves were about fifty years old and ratty-looking — no, mean-looking — no, dumb-looking — no, broken-looking . . .

The woman's eyes met mine. I immediately felt ashamed. "Why don't you go in front of me?" I mumbled, staring at her Hamburger Helper. "You don't seem to have much stuff . . ."

"Nah, that's okay," she said.
"Go on," her man added, meaning that I should start unloading my cart.

Fresh fish, chicken breasts, fresh strawberries, chocolate macaroons and jellies . . . There was no need to place the separator between our orders.

For the entire ride home, I told the kids stories about the Prophet Elijah.

בהר   Leviticus 25—26:2

"'You shall proclaim release throughout the land for all
its inhabitants. It shall be a jubilee for you: each of you
shall return to his holding and each of you shall return
to his family. That fiftieth year shall be a jubilee for
you: you shall not sow, neither shall you reap the
aftergrowth or harvest the untrimmed vines, for it is a
jubilee. It shall be holy to you: you may only eat the
growth direct from the field. . . . And should you ask,
'What are we to eat in the seventh year, if we may
neither sow nor gather in our crops?' I will ordain My
blessing for you in the sixth year, so that it shall yield a
crop sufficient for three years. When you sow in the
eighth year, you will still be eating old grain of that
crop; you will be eating the old until the ninth year,
until its crops come in. But the land must not be sold
beyond reclaim, for the land is Mine; you are but
strangers resident with Me. Throughout the land that
you hold, you must provide for the redemption of the
land.'"

Redemption of the Land

When Moshiach comes. . .
The Pentagon will be a post office.
The President will be in therapy
at least once a week.
The average American will speak three languages
When Moshiach comes.

When Moshiach comes. . .
The National Anthem will be a jazz standard.
The White House will be redecorated
as the Rainbow Room.
We'll proudly fly the flag
When Moshiach comes.

People will often ask, "What day is today?"
It will be fun to stand in line.
We'll all have Bloomingdale's credit cards
When Moshiach comes.

When Moshiach comes. . .
"Fuck you" will be a friendly greeting.
High school kids will be taught
to be attentive lovers.
Tampons and sanitary napkins will be free
When Moshiach comes.

Those who rape will be taught, by men, to weep.
Those who steal will be given what they want.
Those who abuse will be held with loving arms
When Moshiach comes.

"How shall we get rid of our dismantled weapons?"
Who should be the first inducted into the
Hall of Outstanding Gay Americans?
How will we apologize to each other
When Moshiach comes?

When Moshiach comes. . .
Russia will be named Glasnostia
The U.S. will be named the Altered States.
We'll be much, much less afraid
When Moshiach comes.

Africa will host the feast.
Glasnostia will offer the benediction.
The Altered States will receive an invitation
When Moshiach comes.

Israeli arms — and legs — will replace lost limbs in Central America.
The U.N. will declare that "Zionism ain't all that bad."
There will be no weapons in Jerusalem
When Moshiach comes.

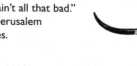

When Moshiach comes. . .
Whales and dolphins will send messages of congratulations.
The only endangered species will be Male Chauvinist Pigs.
We'll still be allowed to kill mosquitos
When Moshiach comes.

We'll proudly display our wrinkles.
We'll notice each other's eyes.
We'll dream less of other worlds
When Moshiach comes.

"I want to share this with my mother."
"I wish my father had lived to see this."
Will there be a resurrection
When Moshiach comes?

When Moshiach comes. . .
We will wonder how long Moshiach intends to stay.
We will try to be brave and stop weeping.
We will forgive but not forget
When Moshiach comes.

בחקתי Leviticus 26:3—27

"'I will grant peace in the land, and you shall lie down
untroubled by anyone; I shall give the land respite from
vicious beasts, and no sword shall cross your land. You
shall give chase to your enemies, and they shall fall before
you by the sword. Five of you shall give chase to a hundred, and a hundred of you shall give chase to ten thousand; your enemies shall fall before you by the sword. I
will look with favor upon you, and make you fertile and
multiply you; and I will maintain my Covenant with you.
You shall eat old grain long stored, and you shall have to
clear out the old to make room for the new.'"

Glory Days

The 1940s in America. . . .

The War was just.
The Hairstyles were A-okay.
Sinatra was in good voice.

And our parents were
still in love.

We're the

Baby Boomers in
Favor of the Forties

"To hell with the Sixties —
let's bring back the Forties!"

Numbers

במדבר   Numbers 1—4:20

"On the first day of the second month, in the second year following the exodus from the land of Egypt, the Lord spoke to Moses in the wilderness of Sinai, in the Tent of Meeting, saying: Take a census of the whole Israelite community by the clans of its ancestral houses. . ."

Names

By way of introduction at the Jewish Reconstructionist convention, we spoke about our names.

Miriam had originally been named Mary, after an aunt who had survived the Holocaust by being given as a young girl to a Polish Catholic family. There were no Jewish relatives left to reclaim her after the war, Miriam reported, and the aunt had been very close to entering a convent when she fell in love with a Jewish intellectual active in the post-war Polish communist government. They married, and Mary Szabolcsi née Miryam Goldfarb became Mary Blumshtayn. They moved to Israel in 1968.

Our latter-day Mary had taken the name Miriam and become a rabbi, she said, "mostly to sort this all out."

Carol, recovering from breast cancer, had been given a new Hebrew name, Simcha, by a Yemenite rabbi in Jerusalem. Simcha, in turn, had committed herself to a new weekly *tzedakah* discipline — to help heal the world, she said.

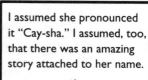

Mordecai, the son of Holocaust survivors and a '60s radical, had renamed himself at the time of the American Bicentennial, after 26 years as "Marvin."

His comrades were troubled by the name change, for fear that he was becoming some kind of "Zionist fascist." Mordecai retorted that his own grandfather had been killed by real fascists — and then he introduced them to the historical figure of Mordecai Anielewitz, leader of the Warsaw Ghetto uprising.

Enid, a lesbian, spoke about how she and her partner were teaching their child to call one of them "Mom" and the other "Mommy."

Enid had been born into an Hassidic family; her own mommy, she said, had abandoned her abusive husband and her children before Enid had even begun to call her mommy "Mom."

Each of our names spoke volumes about history, anti-Semitism, assimilation and recovery. Each story choked me up, in one way or another.

Later, I was buying a candy bar at the hotel gift shop. The cashier was a black woman of about 21 wearing a nameplate as part of her uniform: Keisha.

I assumed she pronounced it "Cay-sha." I assumed, too, that there was an amazing story attached to her name.

But I was too shy to ask . . .

נשא   Numbers 4:21—7

"Thus shall you bless the people of Israel. Say to them:
The Lord bless you and keep you!
The Lord deal kindly and graciously with you!
The Lord bestow His favor upon you and grant you peace!"

Protection

O n the morning of our flight, the family is crazy with rituals.
Susan and I are leaving the kids for a weekend — for the first time in years!

Zoë makes an ink spot on her finger and on Susan's toe.
"You can't take a bath," she warns her mom.
(My sweater pocket still holds the tiny bear she "lent" me
for my last overnight trip, months ago.)

Jonah makes me tie his sneakers for him and insists on having my car key
in his pocket while we're away.

I have already awoken early from horrible dreams about chasing women
and losing body parts. I feel compelled to tell Susan every detail.

UNFINISHED BUSINESS   **UNPROCESSED EMOTIONS**

UNDISCLOSED SECRETS   **UNRESOLVED PROBLEMS**

UNMARKED PROPERTY   **UNTIED SHOELACES**

**ANY OF THESE
CAN UNDO OUR SAFETY.**

At the airport, Susan can't locate her driver's license to present as photo ID.
No big deal — it's not as if she's lost a credit card or the plane tickets,
and the ticket agent is glad to accept another form of ID as proof that
she's not a terrorist — yet Susan seems kind of panicky and breathless . . .

As our plane calls for boarding, she locates the license.
"Whew, now I can rest, finally!" she says.

I glance up at the ceiling: "She doesn't mean that." We both laugh, and off we go.

בהעלתך   Numbers 8—12

"The Lord spoke to Moses in the wilderness of Sinai, on the first new moon of the second year following the exodus from the land of Egypt, saying: Let the Israelite people offer the passover sacrifice at its set time: you shall offer it on the fourteenth day of this month, at twilight, at its set time; you shall offer it in accordance with all its rules and rites."

Multiple Choice Ma Nishtanah

WHY IS THIS NIGHT DIFFERENT FROM ALL OTHER NIGHTS?

a) Because it's Passover, silly!   b) What, different? It's the same every year.

c) Because we stay up doing dishes until three in the morning.

WHY ON THIS NIGHT DO WE EAT UNLEAVENED BREAD?

a) So the supermarket will stock it again next year.   b) What else is there to do with matzoh?

c) Because we're starving, already!

WHY ON THIS NIGHT DO WE EAT BITTER HERBS?

a) For the rush.   b) Nissan is hayfever month.   c) As a chaser for that sweet wine.

WHY ON THIS NIGHT DO WE DIP TWICE?

a) We don't have a swimming pool of our own.   b) Shmutz on the karpas.

c) The drawer was open and it looked so easy.

WHY ON THIS NIGHT DO WE RECLINE AT THE SEDER MEAL?

a) Who has enough chairs for this mob?   b) The Hagadah is too long to sit through.

c) For lack of a vomitorium.

BONUS POINT QUESTIONS

WHY DO WE OPEN THE DOOR FOR ELIJAH?

a) His hands are full.   b) He doesn't have a key.

c) So the anti-Semites can see that we didn't kill any Christian children this time.

WHY DOES PASSOVER ALWAYS COME ON A FULL MOON?

a) It does?   c) So the Angel of Death doesn't make any mistakes.

c) God had plenty of manna but ran out of flashlight batteries.

GIVEN OUR IGNORANCE AND HIGH INTERMARRIAGE RATE, HOW DO YOU EXPECT THE JEWISH PEOPLE TO SURVIVE?

a) Hey, I'm just trying to survive seeing my whole family!   b) Matzoh crumb trails.

c) Can we eat now?

שלח לך   Numbers 13—15

"At the end of forty days they returned from scouting
the land. They went straight to Moses and Aaron and
the whole Israelite community at Kadesh in the wilderness of Paran, and they made their report to them and
to the whole community, as they showed them the fruit
of the land. This is what they told him: 'We came to the
land you sent us to; it does indeed flow with milk and
honey, and this is its fruit. However, the people who
inhabit the country are powerful, and the cities are
fortified and very large . . .'"

And This Is Its Fruit

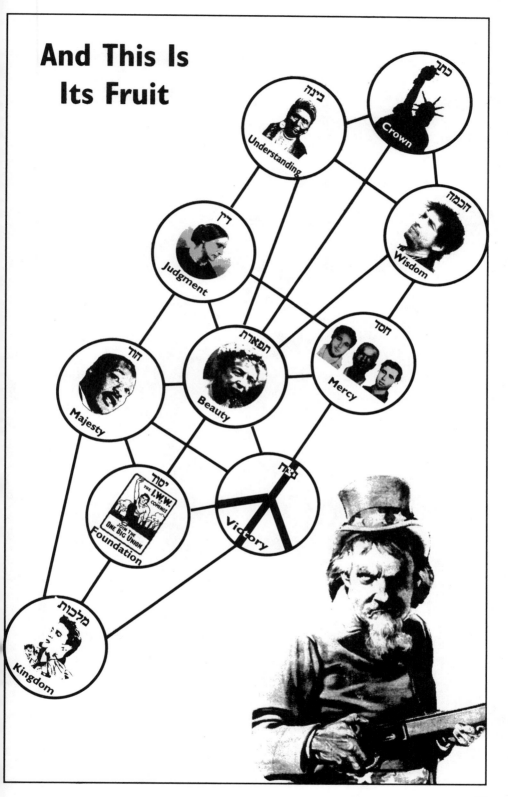

קרח Numbers 16—18

"'Now Korah, son of Izhar son of Kohath son of Levi, betook himself, along with Dathan and Abiram sons of Eliab, and On son of Peleth — descendents of Reuben — to rise up against Moses, together with two hundred and fifty Israelites, chieftains of the community, chosen in the assembly, men of repute. They combined against Moses and Aaron and said to them, 'You have gone to far! For all the community are holy, all of them, and the Lord is in their midst. Why then do you raise your selves above the Lord's congregation?'"

Stardust

Lucy in the sky with diamonds! ♪ ♪

I hadn't gone, supposedly because of my summer job — but actually, I told them, because I was too much of a snob to relate to group scenes.

It must have been the Beatles playing on the CD that got us talking about Woodstock.

I would have resented all those big shots playing music up onstage (and having drugs and sex backstage), I said. I figured I was better off just listening to their music with my girlfriend at home.

"Boy," said my friend Bruce, "you pick the wrong times to feel competitive, you know that?"

I observed that the Fab Four hadn't been there, either. "It wasn't exactly Mt. Sinai," I said.

"No," Bruce said, "but almost. I can't believe you let your ego get in the way of your being there!"

"Eh, just a bunch of idolaters," I muttered, "rolling around in the mud."

"And how!" he said.

חֻקַּת   Numbers 19—22:1

"Whoever touches a corpse, the body of a person who
has died, and does not cleanse himself, defiles the Lord's
Tabernacle; that person shall be cut off from Israel. Since
the water of lustration was not dashed on him, he remains
unclean; his uncleanness is still upon him."

Water of Lustration

For the second Saturday night in a row, it happens. We're watching a video with the kids, and Susan's eyes well with tears at some high point of melodrama.

The kids tease her for being a softie. She laughs, wipes her eyes and says,
"I don't even know why I'm crying!"
"How about Vietnam?" I suggest darkly. "Or Babi Yar. The Atlantic Passage. Cambodia!"
"What do you mean?" Jonah wants to know.
I can't stop listing them. "Rwanda. Bosnia. Cancer. Starvation. Racism. Rape. . . ."
That does it. Susan shuts me up with a look.
"What do you mean?" Jonah still wants to know.
I shake my head. "Just that there's plenty in this world to cry about."
"Like what?" he says, excited for a story, but I wave him off and head to the bathroom.

Nu, Mister, I say to my impassive face in the mirror, *when's the last time you cried?*
Not popcorn tears, but the real thing.
When's the last time that macho mind of yours fled its throne like the petty dictator it is,
leaving you to weep and shake and sob, O God O God O God?

(I sound like my mother when I weep. Afterwards, I get as sleepy as a newborn.)

It has been five years, I calculate. Five years surrounded by corpses (we are all surrounded by corpses), but without the water of lustration. Five years without that core ritual of the circumcised heart: marking our doorpost with tears, to stir God's womb.

I hear Jonah at the bathroom door.
"Dad," he calls in a shy voice, "are you crying?"
"No," I reply, and swing the door open.
"If I were, I'd come out and show you. It's bedtime,"
I add, with a hand on his head. "Get into your peejays
and I'll tell you some stories."

So I do — stories of Rabbi Akiva. Akiva the Genius, who went
from ignoramus to Master Rabbi in 13 years;
Akiva, whom the Talmud calls "father of the world."
One day, I tell my son, Rabbi Akiva sat weeping on the
Sabbath. His disciples were baffled. "Our master," they said,
"you taught us: 'Call the Sabbath a delight.' "

"This is my delight," said Akiva.

בלק   Numbers 22:2—25:9

"While Israel was staying at Shittim, the people profaned
themselves by whoring with the Moabite women, who
invited the people to the sacrifices for their god. The
people partook of them and worshipped that god. Thus
Israel attached itself to Baal-peor, and the Lord was
incensed with Israel. The Lord said to Moses, 'Take all
the ringleaders and have them publicly impaled before
the Lord, so that the Lord's wrath may turn away from
Israel.' So Moses said to Israel's officials, 'Each of you
slay those of his men who attached themselves to Baal-
peor.' . . . Then the plague against the Israelites was
checked. Those who died of the plague numbered twenty-
four thousand."

Please Post Prominently

FIRST AID FOR
SHTUPPING

1 ASK: "Are you shtupping?"

If victim is unconscious or irresponsible. . .

Universal Shtupping Sign

2 Have someone buy LATEX CONDOMS

Important: If person is already using a condom, stand by but do not interfere!

3 If person is **CONSCIOUS** and **RESPONSIBLE**

4

Perform favorite maneuvers 6-10 times.

New York State Department of Intercourse • L.D. Babushkin, Commissioner   Please Post Prominently

פינחס   Numbers 25:10—30:1

"In the seventh month, on the first day of the month, you shall observe a sacred occasion: you shall not work at your occupations. You shall observe it as a day when the horn is sounded. . . . On the tenth day of the same seventh month you shall observe a sacred occasion when you shall practice self-denial. You shall do no work. You shall present to the Lord a burnt offering of pleasing odor . . ."

Holiday Cerebrations

When American holidays roll around, I feel very Jewish.

At Thanksgiving, I identify more with the Native Americans than with the Pilgrims.

At Halloween, I mourn for women burned at the stake as witches by the same Inquisitors who burned Jews.

Marching with the flag on July 4th seems kind of idolatrous to me.

When Jewish holidays roll around, I feel very American.

At Passover, I think more about the Underground Railroad than about the Sea of Reeds.

At Hanukah, I fret about religious fanaticism and intolerance of the kind exemplified by the Maccabees.

So does dancing with the Torah on Simchat Torah.

Add to all this my overly rational personality, my distaste for crowds, my workaholism and my dilapidated wardrobe, and you get the picture: I'm a holiday-challenged person!

**Fellow Americans:
Only a few weeks lef** until
THE DAY OF ATONEMEN
**This Space Available
for Public Apologies**

Join the many outstanding world leaders and personaliti will be offering messages of guilt, contrit and atoneme along America's highways this Autumn.
**YOU CAN APOLOGIZE TO/FOR ANYONE. IT DOESN'T EVEN HAV BE
YOUR FAULT!**

מטות   Numbers 30:2—32

"The amount of booty, other than the spoil that the troops had plundered, came to 675,000 sheep, 72,000 head of cattle, 61,000 asses, and a total of 32,000 human beings, namely, the women who had not had carnal relations."

Birth of a Nation

"Can we ordain to ourselves the awful
majesty of God — to decide what
cities and villages are to be destroyed,
who will live and who will die, and
who will join the refugees wandering
in a desert of our own creation?"
— Robert F. Kennedy, 1968

מסעי   Numbers 33—36

"When you cross the Jordan into the land of Canaan,
you shall dispossess all the inhabitants of the land. . ."

Sez Who?

She wants self-determination. . .

and something more.

intifadah

The Scent of Rebellion

Deuteronomy

דברים   Deuteronomy 1—3:22

"Moreover, your little ones who you said would be carried off, your children who do not yet know good from bad, they shall enter it; to them will I give it and they shall possess it."

Little People of the Book

ואתחנן　Deuteronomy 3:23—7:11

"For I the Lord your God am an impassioned God,
visiting the guilt of the parents upon the children, upon
the third and upon the fourth generations. . ."

Hard Time

I'm driving home at night from the Public Speaking class that I teach at Downstate Correctional Facility.

The last class is scheduled for December 23rd — two weeks from tonight, and only two days before Christmas. I've already told the guys that my son is scheduled to be born by then!

As I drive through the darkness, I fantasize bringing my newborn son into the prison on the 23rd.

Hey, no kidding!

Good luck, Mr. Babushkin.

Man, I haven't seen my kids in a dog's age!

It's their final speaking assignment. . .

. . . TO BLESS THIS CHILD!

Don't use any dirty needles, kid.

Peace, little brother.

Make a lot of money.

Tell your old man to treat you right or he'll answer to me!

Don't grow up too fast.

Stay out of this place, for sure.

The next morning, I call to ask the head of security: Might I bring an infant into the facility for just a few minutes?

No good, he says —

Too much of a security risk!

עקב   **Deuteronomy 7:12—11:25**

"Take care lest you forget the Lord your God and fail to
keep His commandments, His rules, and His laws,
which I enjoin upon you today. When you have eaten
your fill, and have built fine houses to live in, and your
herds and flocks have multiplied, and your silver and
gold have increased, and everything you own has pros-
pered, beware lest your heart grow haughty. . ."

Babylon Talmud

ראה   Deuteronomy 11:26—16:17

"For there will never cease to be needy ones in your
land, which is why I command you: open your hand to
the poor and needy kinsman in your land."

Windshield Wiper

SKID ROW

Rabbi Yehudah used to say:
Ten strong things were created in the world —
A mountain is strong, but iron cuts through it.
Iron is strong, but fire causes it to bubble.
Fire is strong, but water extinguishes it.
Water is strong, but clouds contain it.

Breath is strong, but the body holds it in.
The body is strong, but fear breaks it.
Fear is strong, but wine dissipates it.
Wine is strong, but sleep overcomes it.
Death is harder than all of them.
But *tsedakah* saves from death,
as it is written. . .

—Bava Batra 10a

103

שפטים   Deuteronomy 16:18—21:9

"You shall not move your countryman's landmarks, set up by previous generations, in the property that will be allotted to you in the land that the Lord your God is giving you to possess."

BY PRESIDENTIAL PROCLAMATION

National
Mimeograph
Remembrance
Week

September 18—25

U.S. COMMITTEE FOR LANDMARK TECHNOLOGIES

William Gates, *President*
Dr. Emmanuel Typewriter, *Immediate Past President*
Mr. and Mrs. Rex and Mimi O'Graph
Mrs. Gus Stetner

כי תצא   Deuteronomy 21:10—25

"'[W]hen the Lord your God grants you safety from all your enemies around you . . . you shall blot out the memory of Amalek from under heaven. Do not forget!'"

Bad Dream

Again, the same: I'm walking through the street, headed somewhere or other, and all of a sudden I realize that I'm dressed only in my underpants! The humiliation is awful — the horror of being seen, being caught — yet nobody seems to notice . . . What's the matter with these people?

And what's the matter with me? I'm a middle-aged man! Why am I still having such adolescent dreams?

כי תבוא   Deuteronomy 26—29:8

"All these blessings shall come upon you and take effect,
if you will but heed the word of the Lord your God:

Blessed shall you be in the city and blessed shall you
be in the country.

Blessed shall be the issue of your womb, the produce
of your soil, and the offspring of your cattle, the calving
of your heard and the lambing of your flock.

Blessed shall be your basket and your kneading bowl.

Blessed shall you be in your comings and blessed shall
you be in your goings."

Smell the
Coffee

"All the News That's Fit to Print"

The New York Times

LATE CITY EDITION
Weather: Clear, getting better all day. Details, p. 44

VOL. CXLIX .... No. 51,754   NEW YORK, SATURDAY, JANUARY 1, 2000   FREEBIE TODAY

EARTH OBSERVES MILLENNIUM WITH WORLDWIDE JUBILATION; TRUCE ON ARMED CONFLICT WILL BE EXTENDED "INDEFINITELY"

Outside Gates of Jerusalem, Last Known Nuclear Devices Are Buried

Children with Shovels Complete Disarmament

L.D. BABUSHKIN

Outside Herod's Gate, Jerusalem, the bomb burial took place

Jerusalem, Jan. 1 —
of schoolchildr
every contin
ered at day
the ancie
usale
b

Israel, the
er its nuclear
ly recently was

achanting, drumming
Buddhist monks, Jew-
uns and priests, Native
ican holy men and other
ers and religious leaders
member nations of the U.N.,
10 children, representatives

The Earth

Fortune 500 Companies Dedicate 50% of Profits to Cancer Research

Chemical Giants Lead Effort for Answers

L.D. BABUSHKIN

1 — A new consor-
ns with combined as-
more than $12 trillion
dged today to devote 50%
their annual profits to the
"prevention and cure of the cancer scourge within the decade."
Initiated by the environmental
activist organization, Green-
peace, and several giants of the
chemical and oil industries, the
consortium, Earth-Group, Inc.,
will make its first assessment on
participating corporations in
time to present a check at United
Nations headquarters here in
time for Earth Day, 2001. That
payment, expected to total $95
billion, will be repeated on a
semi-annual basis "until our
planet is restored to the kind of
pristine condition it was in when

fund will be administered
by the United Nations
Earth Intelligence Founda-
(Continued on p. 12)

A Date Awaited in Dread Proves Joyous

L.D. BABUSHKIN

New York, Jan.   The arrival
of the ye   ied
meaning
nations,
calenda
planet, b
universall
relief. "We
said United N
tary-General M
in a pre-dawn state
U.N. headquarters her
"We face the future as a t
united, truly liberated human
race."
    Ms. Chee announced that the
international truce on armed
conflict that has been in place
since Jan. 1, 1999 has not seen
a violation for nine months and
has been "extended indefi-
nitely" by the General Assembly. "Partnership, not domi-
nance, is now the force of history," Ms. Chee said in a state-
ment accompanying the an-

tions, festivals and porten-
tous proclamations and an-
nouncements marked the
day as the kind of redemp-
event that many Chris-
ssianists nnouncing
uries. In Rome,
d on behalf of
atholic.
apology to
en sub-
ame
n-
P
off
gy to
nation
native p
Other rel
urged relig
"eschew tri
and see our
binding toge

INSIDE

Kissinger Dies in Hanoi
Former war criminal spent final years in Viet- nam's capital working intensively on refolia- tion efforts. **Page 24.**

¡Play Ball! Havana to Receive Major League Franchise

Gay Museum to Induct Three
The newest museum on the Mall inducts Walt Whit- man, Bessie Smith, Bayard Rustin. **Page 33.**

Yiddish Book Tops Bestseller List for 3rd Week
The first Yiddish block-

New Name fo Exxon: "Moxi
CEO announces plan to "decentralize and humanize" corporate

South Africa Announces Creation of Food Bank

נצבים   Deuteronomy 29:9—30

"Surely, this Instruction which I enjoin upon you this day is not too baffling for you, nor is it beyond reach. It is not in the heavens, that you should say, 'Who among us can go up to the heavens and get it for us and impart it to us, that we may observe it?' Neither is it beyond the sea, that you should say, 'Who among us can cross to the other side of the sea and get it for us and impart it to us, that we may observe it?' No, the thing is very close to you, in your mouth and in your heart, to observe it."

הכנסת אורחים	תפלה	כשרות
Hospitality	Prayer	Keeping Kosher
צדקה	מנורה	שלום
Economic Justice	Menorah	Peace
למוד	שלום בית	כלל ישראל
Study	Household Harmony	Jewish Unity

Judaism is in Your Hands

וַיֵּלֶךְ **Deuteronomy 31**

"The Lord said to Moses: The time is drawing near for
you to die. Call Joshua and present yourselves in the
Tent of Meeting, that I may instruct him."

S.W.A.K.

Sometimes when I glimpse the adults emergent in my children's faces,
I am suddenly whisked to my death bed.

My wife has already died. I am very old, very weak, and very conscious.
Zoë and Jonah are at my side, waiting for my blessing.

They are good people. They have accomplished much. I have no useful advice to offer.
The world outside is worse in some ways, better in others. I have no prophecy to offer.
Every belief I have held has proved flawed and inadequate. I have no wisdom to offer.

So I tell them a story.
It's the story of Moses' death —
how no angel, not even the Angel of Death, was willing or able to obey God's will,
and separate Moses' soul from his body.
Finally the Holy One came down to do it, saying,
"Daughter . . ." (and here I choke up) —
"Daughter, the time of your sojourn in the body of Moses has ended . . ."

Then God kissed Moshe Rabbenu, and the Soul rushed forth in ecstasy!

Now I smile at Zoë and point to my old, wrinkled cheek.
She bends and gives me a soft kiss.

I turn to Jonah and point to my other cheek.
He bends and gives me a kiss
(such delicious lips).

"Being your father," I tell them,
"has been my greatest fulfillment."

And I feel my soul rushing, rushing . . .

האזינו   Deuteronomy 32

" 'They incensed Me with no-gods,
Vexed Me with their futilities;
I'll incense them with a no-folk,
 Vex them with a nation of fools.' "

115

וזאת הברכה　Deuteronomy 33—34

"With the bounty of dew from heaven, / And of the deep that couches below; / With the bounteous yield of the sun, / And the bounteous crop of the moons. . ."

This Is the Blessing

My wife is a land of milk and honey,

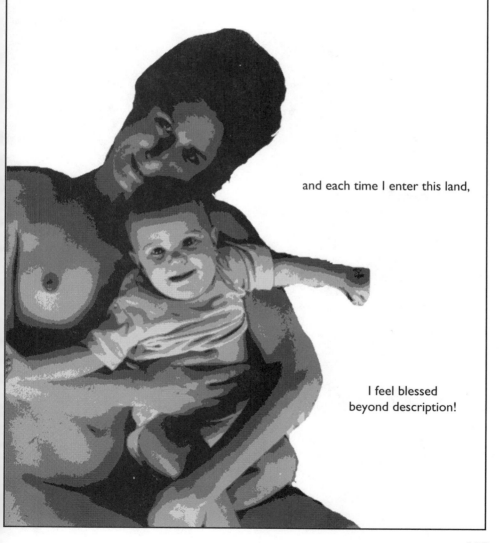

and each time I enter this land,

I feel blessed
beyond description!

List of Torah Portions

About the Author

Lawrence Bush is a novelist and essayist who has been joining word and image together for the past number of years, much of it sent out as "mail art" under the name *Babushkin's Digest*. He edits *Reconstructionism Today*, the magazine of the Jewish Reconstructionist Federation, and serves as a communications consultant for several other Jewish organizations. Bush is author of three books of fiction and co-author of the resource book, *Jews, Money and Social Responsibility*. His stories and essays have been published in the *New York Times, Village Voice, Tikkun, Moment,* and *MAD* magazine, among other publications.